SKALD

SKALD

Skald
Sword & Sea-Cloud

Ian Crockatt

2020

Published by Arc Publications,
Nanholme Mill, Shaw Wood Road
Todmorden OL14 6DA, UK
www.arcpublications.co.uk

978 1908376 80 0

Design by Tony Ward
Cover illustration by Wenna Crockatt
Printed in the UK by Ashford, Gosport, Hants

*In memory of
my twin sister Gill*

ACKNOWLEDGEMENTS

The complete text of SKALD was originally published
in *Poetry Scotland* issues 43 & 46. It was first published
in chapbook form in 2009 by Koo Press, and reprinted
by them in 2011. 'Viking Spring' was also published
in the anthology *New Writing Scotland 25*

Arc Pamphlet Series
Series Editor: Tony Ward

CONTENTS

I
Widow

VIKING SPRING

This: barley green as grass
   swaying in gusty May;
its clouds of brandished blades.
   This: ghost-blurs from the coast,
hoar-brained crows cawing, haar
   fingering the halting
hearts and limbs of lambs
   willed to life on the hill.

And this: wing-whirr of geese,
   wind-arrows in narrow
formation confirming
   sea-currents still foment
their baleful heat, hot blood
   and gold-greed still breed in
the mind; sea-wolves still found
   fine steel in hearts: yours; mine.

LANGUAGE

Language, teased from his tongue,
  snared, tangled as his hair,
invades her inner ear.
  Finding it floods her mind
with oath, sinew, saga
  she rejects it, objects,
claims testosterone-tossed
  words do *this*: turns, kisses

him – so softly, so calm
  in her certainty, her
intimate mouth-lore, that
  his brushed lips let hers slip
moth-winged by. What cloud-flung
  thousand-watt bolt so jolts
the mind, sends such insect-
  fine tremors down our spines?

CUIL SOUND

Sea-rider stalks the red
   throat of dawn, sheer-bowed boat
heaving the west-bound waves
   North, South of her. Wet-mouthed
cold Cuil Sound flings sea-cloud,
   hails salt-scales, harries her,
hisses, hoards sore kisses
   for the heart-wood of her.

It's not hard to make it
   out, the frail half-heard shout
of life-fall, fallible,
   candle-flame small. What hand
stayed there on my dark dear's
   shoulder when dusk rolled her
into eternity –
   keel-band, tall mast and all?

The old Gods gone ga-ga
   in the loft; the glad, soft
crucified one crying
   from steeples, Christendom
spreading its bloodstains all
   over sweet Earth. What's worth
sighing for – my sea-wolf
   up-keeled, drowned, in Cuil Sound?

HIS RING

Not gold – gilt silver that
   glowed like those gleam-haloed
stone-encrusted crosses
   grabbed from Christ-cold abbeys
in southern isles; his scythe
   in fields of yielding oats
braiding circles of light; not
   death-willed – breath-filled, ice-bright.

Is this progress? Live limbs
  split like strakes on unlit
rock, the sun rolling back
  the hours to that rich, soured
dawn, him adoring our
  unborn futures, putting
his ear to our hearts? Your
  father hacked the kelp-path

from now to nowhere – rock-
  riven – strong-kneed then, long-
backed, hair black as the tar
  he smeared on her planks, clear
eye bright as the night-sky
  possessed by stars. At best
the sea-whelped wave of love
  persists: we kiss, we part.

CUIL CLIFFS

The wall of Cuil cliff is
   crammed with gannets, jammed in
cracks or lodged on ledges,
   wedged in wave-lashed caves. Flight,
and their slick vertical
   stoop through the arcs and scoops
of deflected seas act
   on imaginations

as tongue-tips do on spines –
   may such ardent touchings
deluge and delight you.
   The debt the gannet owes
to these seas implies each
   possesses awareness.
No, they're sapped and *now*-swept
   as my sea-wolf's love-cry.

THE UNPROTECTED

Now that a thin sleet-smirr
  sogs the horse's coat, force-
feeds itself through door-slats
  and loose-thatched straw-patched roofs,
we're anyone's; wolves, skalds, elves
  crossed monks, weirds, berserks, lost
gods – bastards all – enthral
  us. Child, welcome to hell.

DROWNING

I love you, moon. I'd give
   my two breasts to hold you.
Sky-rider, when your dream
   lets you down drown with me
in the vague haar of my hair
   on this blue heath beneath
you. Moon, do you doubt me?
   Here's my tear-washed shadow.

PLEA

Bequeather of slain stars,
  of bombarded atoms,
science and sorcery,
  high, silver-dotted sky-
fuls of massed gases, gild
  the grave's dark socket, save
our minds from its earth-bound
  thin-ice-bright finale –

lance-shards of light, planets
  dead beyond them, headlong
flight of debris through night
  and night of nothing, white-
out behind the eyes. Fate,
  expose each explosive
fact that proves wrecked souls can
  thole the whole smashed shebang.

SWANS

As if crow-caw and gale
   were all. After word came
of his tumble through time,
   soul-bells tolling the hour,
thunder-blue cloud-towers
   coursing the mind, she cursed
that beach, that *sloven's snatch,*
   that *whore's-mouth* of a shore –

licked lip of land, tongue-tip-
   flicked Cuil peninsula,
gashed, anemone-gummed,
   sand-filled saliva gland
with all the deep-throat thrills
   of a doused forge… gorged then
on heart, did you – she howls
   through wave-fall, gale, grief, all –

soused hero in your maw?
   Today Cuil Sound plays 'swans
neck' in her glass, finesse-
   cum-suppleness, couples
their charmed white stalks – *wound limbs*
   of my sea-wolf's bride – hides
each to its nape in duped
   waters; lust's – death's – daughters.

WIDOW

The doo'cot back of Cuil
  Loan becomes a war-zone
when she leans light bones on
  it – shadowy, sunlit –
shifting beneath her shift,
  gleam-haloed sheaves of hair,
willing her hawk-winged mind
  to love white doves to death.

RAINBOW

arc of the arrow
    from
  goatskin to shot silk

arc of the arrow
    from
  flint to titanium

arc of the arrow
    from
  beast-gods to atheism

arc of the arrow
    from
  stumble to arabesque

arc of the arrow
    from
  rationalist to lover

arc of the arrow
    from
  ravager to asylum

arc of the arrow
    from
  kernel to acreage

arc of the arrow
    from
  void to kaleidoscope

arc of stark illusion
   bridge of giddy droplets
mighty prism of sighs

arc of the arrow
     from
birth-pain to headstone

eyebrow of
 earth's green eye

ENQUIRER

This scuffed scarecrow – this cough-
  ing tatter-breeks streaked with
spring rain – grins, asks direct-
  ions to our earl's hall. Burly
though, teeth straight as the jaw-
  bones they jut from; but not
just that – how to not not-
  ice nerved eyes, dawdling thighs..

GHOSTS

These barley-packed parks. Crows
   flying plumed crosses high
over our spear-crowded
   acres. Other word-makers
mouth myths at the cliff's edge
   where gull-squalls mewl and trawl,
skiffs founder, drowned men loll
   their logged limbs ashore. Your

words feel real, rebuilding
   the flesh of event, fresh
as dawn-dew, raw as brawn
   in a blood-pool, heart-full.
When ghosts of the past un-
   hinge me, when fears impinge
broken-limbed sea-wolves, strakes
   wrenched from keels, more wracked men,

stay, lie between my breasts
   hearing the life-blood flood
through muscled pipe and pump,
   tell me the plunging swell's
murmur is a mirage,
   the mimetic whimper
of some hurt outcast, lost,
   found, bound, high-shouldered home.

II
Raiders

TOASTS

To consanguinity!
   Sons and more sons! Tonnage
of curved strakes and carved keels!
   Hide-jerkinned berserkers!
Hard dyed-in-wolf's-blood blades!
   Our Earl's skiff's steam-bent beams!
Sea-roads! Gold! Honeyed mead!
   Slave-girls' mouths! Southerlies!

WAITING

The hall waits; a silo
   listening for launched missiles:
hurled keels cresting cold seas.
   Wheesht, heart, terror unleashed
is simply a stored dream
   of swung blades, flung firebrands,
thatch spitting, glass splitting,
   mind-seams parting; your dream,

your blues, your slow-worm fuse
   sparking the dark, switching
its lit tail to and fro.
   Theirs too – may their snared guts
re-coil, turn cannibal,
   cold spine fluids shudder,
torn from dreams by sirens,
   tom-tom riffs, cliff-top fires.

AFTERMATH

Paul Scorff's soul was wounded.
   Mouths rave – in his skull's cave
axe-scars' fixed grins open,
   cursing serpents burst out;
his skin's white, unbroken.
   Garth's leg's irregular
gouts of blood had him eat-
   ing screams. Urf stutters reams

of moon-struck verse. Venn
   twirls snivelling girls on
his thigh-stump. Cold camp fires,
   the torpor of corpses,
that slapstick raven-strut
   of drunken monk-slayers.
Under the rowan – spell-
   bound – my eyes welled, drowned me.

LOVE, SCARS

I know these mute scars, how
    their marks were gained one dark
hour on the forest floor
    when pell-mell raiders fell
on you as wolf-packs do
    on inconsolable
doe lingering too long
    in dusk's musk-filled lair; I

know how they appeared – as
    arrows from nowhere. So
shy, so seeming-scared, scarred,
    unbelieving – Sweet, weave
my hands through the warm weft
    of your hair, lose your wish-
ing-well mouth to mine in
    the blood-mad shadows of

this warrior-band's brand-
    fire, walk the viewless wire
of heretic love. My
    sword, my heart, my word-hoard –
all yours, whose limbs curve as
    sweetly as taut bows. One
kiss – this, and this – for each
    scar; these for each eye's star.

HORIZONS

When huge waves heave over
 our horizons what dies?
Logic's hegemony?
 Our love of straight lines? Swate
that uphaul, the halliard's
 tension, when her high prow
tracks down the wave-trough. Hope
 no trenail starts or fails

when snow-combers foaming
 crests rise – freeze – capsize
on the flinching crew. Who'd
 forgo the ice-blue flow
of memory – careened
 hulls, the wintering Mulls,
Alba's miles of coast; cave,
 kyle, sea-loch, ransacked isle?

Uncover earth's corners,
 Son, thole those oceans. We
have adapted best – seed-
 sowers, blade-smelters,
proven keel-carvers, star-
 plotters. Helmsman, declaim
the sweep-oar's song – *larboard,*
 starboard, Plunderer run.

ICE

The shock of it – blue-black,
    emerald – blocks, towers,
spires, knife-blades, needles – all
    agony to the eye
and salt-mapped lung. Men wept,
    months-drowned minds were tined,
gaffed and hoisted glistening
    from their depths cell by cell.

CHIMERAS

The swirl and wash and pearl-
   hard water-drops whacked yards
by frenzied whale-pods; up-
   ended flailing tail-flukes
decimating glimpsed cod-
   shoals in these polar seas:
mind-thrill over matter;
   fraught theatres of thought.

cause

dreamers wake to re-draw
their drifting horizons
dawn
the setting of sails

faith

unbelievable gods
battle for both sides' minds
dawn
the setting of sails

loyalty

love the invisible
leads legions of lovers
dawn
the setting of sails

struggle

understanding grapples
with growing conviction
dawn
the setting of sails

hope

aren't miracles manna
to the open-minded?
dawn
the setting of sails

pain

nothing prepares the wound
for a father's anguish
dawn
the setting of sails

regret   home is that half-mirage
                    on the other side of
                          dawn
                    the setting of sails

outcome   noon dusk and midnight lie
                    on the field of lost limbs
                        death
                    the furling of sails

LAND

Heard from the yard-arm
    above us all – shove and
haul of blood in our heads,
    vice of ice in each brain –
the call, Tor's bellow, *land,*
    land to the west, there, west,
blue as the blue whale's hump.
    The shock of it – blues-blue,

frail in the mind's scaled eye,
    shifting, salt-grain-sifting
troubling line, loaned but ours,
    this lost mass discovered
beyond where men's minds go
    – Garth's, Urf's, Paul's, Venn's, Tor's – more
welcome even than found
    wigwammed America.

LAND-LOCKED

Glaciers, volcanoes;
   heat underfoot, iced eyes.
Not spires, spouting geysers;
   the froth and splother of
pulsing mud-pools; sagas;
   fire-gods; unshod ponies'
hooves hacking through muck – yet
   here, my new-found dear, are

thought-perfected acts of
   love; tongues, limbs – yours, mine – twined
tight as splicing-rope. What
   if half the crew are laugh-
ing out loud, 'mad' widow of
   Cuil Sound? My hope-bound mind
urges our hauled keel south,
   south to your arms, your mouth.

HARVEST

Gold-lust's harvest; gowling
   girls for ballast. Fast as
a torpedo – our oars
   rhythmic arc and dip, lick
and slaver of wave-silk
   kissing the keel. Seal-fat-
dripping, whey, honey; bone-
   green haunch, hard dough – pardon

us while we spew…Full-and-
   by lie the skerries of
Faroe – Old Dragon-Toes –
   and the sky's stacked high as
her cliffs with gales of gulls.
   Our dying lie gasping,
already riding their
   last havering waves home

to consanguinity,
   sons and more sons, tonnage
of curved strakes and carved keels,
   hide-jerkinned berserkers,
hard dyed-in-wolf's-blood blades,
   our Earl's skiff's steam-bent beams,
sea-roads, gold, honeyed mead,
   slave-girls' mouths, southerlies.

AFTERWORD

The form used in this series of poems is derived from a highly wrought form developed by the Skalds, professional poets employed by the kings and earls of the Viking courts of the 9th-13th centuries. The Skalds knew which side their bread was buttered – they primarily recorded their patrons' victories in battle and sang the praises of fallen heroes.

Much of their most original work was orally composed in a form called *dróttkvætt*, meaning 'suitable for reciting at court'. Its dense patterns of syllabic internal rhyme and half-rhyme, alliteration and pronounced rhythms, and vivid use of multiple metaphor-like word-pictures called kennings, was perhaps a way of helping them remember it, but over time the Skalds developed *dróttkvætt* into a prized art-form demanding formidable feats of skill and mental dexterity when performed before the court. The poems were passed down the centuries by word of mouth, and most were not written down until the 13th century when they became important and integral features of the Icelandic sagas.

It is a poetry which in places records, and by rights should have become, part of the heritage of the British Isles, one of the many branches of the linguistic and cultural root-system from which English language poetry has grown. When I came across it, initially in academic translations, I loved the intense physicality of the music it hinted at, its combination of compactness and raw energy. The idea of developing a functional English language equivalent for today proved irresistible.

In this series I therefore aimed to replicate the complex features of the *dróttkvætt* form while maintaining an approachable and immediate experience for the modern English-speaking reader.

To get closer to the sound and feel of the 'skaldic' effects, try reading the poems out loud.

It seemed natural to make a quasi Viking tale, set in the landscapes and seascapes of territories once partially or wholly under Viking control – the West Coast of Scotland where I used to live, the north-east corner of Scotland where I live now, and, in one or two poems, Iceland. The form may be new to some, but the emotional landscape will be familiar to all.

Ian Crockatt

BIOGRAPHICAL NOTE

IAN CROCKATT is a prize-winnning poet and poetry translator, who lives in a croft in north-east Scotland with his wife, the ceramic artist and printmaker, Wenna Crockatt.

He has published six collections of his own poetry, and his poem sequence *Original Myths*, with etchings by the Scottish artist Paul Fleming, was nominated for the Saltire Society's Scottish Book of the Year Award in 2000.

As a translator, he won the prestigious Schlegel-Tiek Prize for translation from German in 2014 for *Pure Contracdiction: Selected Poems of Rainer Maria Rilke* (Arc, 2012), and in the same year, his *Crimsoning the Eagle's Claw: Viking Poems of Rognvaldr Kali Kolsson, Earl of Orkney* (Arc, 2014) was a Poetry Book Society Recommended Translation. In 2017, another of his translations from Old Norse, *The Song Weigher: The Complete Poems of Egill Skallagrímsson* was published by Arc.